Thank-you for your support.

MW00907425

STEPPING OUT OF THE BOX

A Journey of Faith

Dian Dames Knight

Dian D. Knight

May 2012

ISBN: 978-1-105-59687-2

Front Page Design by: Cookiesncream Creation

Acknowledgements

To God be the glory for the things he has done!

To my amazing husband Kendall, you are my knight in shining armor, your love for God and people call me higher.

To my sons Joshua and Caleb, Mom loves you very much and looks forward to the noble men of God you are developing into.

To my sister Danielle, thank you for your hard work and creative talents that made this book possible.

To my Mom and Dad, thank you for the legacy of Faith you handed down to our family.

To my sister Yvonne and my brother Michael, thank you for your love and support all these years.

To Nancy Berry thank you for your help in editing the manuscript.

Foreword

I have had the honor of knowing Dian Knight for many years and simply put, she is "More than a conquer". Dian has a God given passion for calling women of all ages, races and backgrounds to step out of the box and allow God to do more than they could ask or imagine. You will be inspired as she beautifully and vulnerably shares about her journey through the good and the challenging times in life. You will also glean nuggets of wisdom from both the scriptures and her personal experiences of stepping out of her box spiritually, academically, professionally, physically and emotionally. I hope that after reading this book, you too will get the courage to step out and believe you can be more than a conqueror.

~Shawn Patterson,

Women's Ministry Leader for Greater Atlanta Church of Christ

Table of Contents

Chapter 1 – The Early Years

*I praise you because I am fearfully and wonderfully made...**Psalm 139:14-17***

I was born August 22, 1958 in Liberty City (Miami), Florida.
My father and mother are both descendants of Bahamians. My father was born in the town of the Ferry, Little Exuma on March 14, 1933. My mother was born in Miami (Overtown) on June 6, 1933, but her mother and father were born on Cat Island in the Bahamas.

My childhood was full of security and stability. My parents raised me and my siblings in a home full of love and full of faith. We were committed members of our local church and I saw no contradictions from what was taught at church and what was lived out at home during my formative years. I always knew and felt loved and believed in. As a result of seeing the bible lived out in front of me it laid a foundation for me to accept it as true and reasonable. My days were full of fun in the sun, school, church activities, piano lessons, and family times on the beach. There were lots of outings with cousins and aunts and uncles.

I participated in many oratory contests, piano recitals, musicals, and later in high school, concert choir performances. Life for me was very predictable:

Sunday - church, Monday –school/homework, Tuesday – school/homework/youth church, Wednesday –school/homework/piano lesson, Thursday – school/homework, Friday – school/homework/youth choir, Saturday – chores/playtime. Once I got into high school, there were choir performances and dates on Saturdays and some Sundays.

I am one of the blessed ones, in that my childhood involved very little drama or trauma. I can remember only a few times of distress. The first time was in kindergarten. The husband of the owner of the kindergarten shot her and then himself. He died and she was paralyzed for life. After that incident I was moved to another kindergarten.

The second was at the beginning of my junior high school days. I was among many African-American children during the 60's who were bused out of our own neighborhoods to begin integrating the school system. I remember the first day of school like it was yesterday. My friends and I boarded the bus and began to talk about what we were about to experience, going to school with kids from the white and Jewish communities. We were all afraid but covered it up by talking tough. If anyone bothered us or spoke to us the wrong way, they would regret it. It was such a relief to have that day go very well. There were some afterschool fights between blacks and whites and Hispanics, but I was never involved in any of that. I actually made some great friends from other cultures. I learned that people are people and that I was no different from my white, Jewish and Hispanic counterparts.

I do remember one situation when I was invited to one of my Jewish friends' homes on one of the islands in between mainland Miami and Miami Beach. My mother kept asking me if I was sure that my friend's parents knew I was coming and if I was okay about going. I did not realize until I became an adult that she was nervous about what I would encounter in this new environment. Needless to say, I had a blast! I visited two of my other classmates as well that day. I remember their homes were a little larger than mine and the rooms were expertly decorated. I did see a difference in lifestyle, but it was a small one. I grew up in what would have been and still is the "hood," but my parents' income was probably middle to upper middle class. I had everything I needed growing up and a whole lot of what I wanted. I never went without food, clothing or shelter. I had regular medical and dental appointments and was loved and cherished and supported from infancy to adulthood. I am still blessed with all of that right now and more!

As I reflect on the life lesson of learning that as human beings we are all the same on the inside, even though our outer coverings are different; I recall Psalm 139:14 where David says we are remarkably and wonderfully made. I am glad that I was able to learn this truth early. This allowed me to embrace the call later in my life to make disciples of Jesus from all nations. Have you embraced this truth? If so, what led you to do so? If not, why not?

My high school years were spent back in my own neighborhood, at Miami Jackson Senior High School. I wanted to attend this high school because I wanted to be a part of their excellent choral program. I had been singing in my church choir, and now I wanted to study vocal performing more seriously.

I will never forget the change in my voice after the summer of my sophomore year in high school. I participated in a summer choral workshop with Roscoe Speed (my choral director at Jackson). This allowed me to have private voice lessons for the first time. I learned the basics of breath support and vocal production that summer and continued to develop my voice. Mr. Speed left Jackson after that summer, but the program was taken over by one of his protégés, Leslie Thomas. Mr. Thomas is the reason I decided to major in vocal performance at the University of Miami in Coral Gables, Florida.

This decision was influenced by Mr. Thomas challenging my resolve at the time to become a nurse. I was a part of a science program preparing minority students for a career in medicine. My aunt Ruth was a nurse so I figured I would follow in her footsteps. I will never forget the day he asked me, "Are you going to sing to your patients?" In that moment he caused me to decide what type of life I would lead; one of status quo or one of adventure. An African-American opera singer was definitely an out of the box musical career choice. I chose adventure and what an amazing ride it has been so far. How will you live from this day forward? A life of adventure is available!

I graduated salutatorian of my class at Jackson and went on to pursue my career as a classical singer. This was the beginning of me stepping out of the box and walking by faith, not by sight
(2 Cor. 5:7).

Lessons learned:

Oratory skill/piano/choir
I liked performing for an audience, and I felt at home on the stage
I learned that people are people, no matter the ethnicity.
I learned to follow my dreams and to dream BIG!
I also learned that there is a God and that the Bible was true and reasonable.

To Do

Journal about the lessons you learned during your childhood, both positive and negative.

_____
_____
_____
_____
_____
_____
_____
_____
_____
_____
_____
_____
_____
_____
_____
_____
_____

Chapter 2 – University of Miami

*It is good to praise the Lord and make music to your name, O Most High...**Psalm 92***

Life during these next four years would prove to be adventurous, exciting, mind-stretching and full of new experiences. I was privileged to receive a half-scholarship to the School of Music at the University of Miami. My high school choral director prepared me very well and my audition went great. Since I had played piano from the age of seven I did a good job on the theory and keyboard tests. I received amazing vocal instruction from Mary Buckley.

She was considered the top vocal teacher at the university at the time, and had prepared many students to go on to sing at the Metropolitan Opera House. She was very protective of her students and monitored how much choral and ensemble singing we were involved in. I was only able to sing with the University of Miami Chamber Singers for one year because of that.

The Chamber Singers were the premier vocal ensemble for the school, and singing with this group allowed you to travel extensively. The year that I was involved we traveled around the country and to Russia. This was a trip of a lifetime! I will never forget those two weeks. It was amazing to travel halfway around the world and meet people from another culture. We sang at different venues, including the Riga Conservatory of Music. It was wonderful to hear their musicians and to be able to share the love of music with them.

Our last concert in Moscow was the most memorable. This was the late 70's, so the freeing up of the Russian government had not yet occurred. We were told that we could not sing the words to any of our sacred songs. Our director, Dr. Kjelson, directed us to sing one of our sacred songs without words, using different vowels. That evening was probably the most perfect rendition of the music we had ever done. Singing that song, knowing the words but not being allowed the freedom to sing them, brought a whole new energy to the music. We understood that night what being free as Americans meant. We all returned home with a greater appreciation for our country. America has had its problems and its shames but we were and ever will be working to form a more perfect union.

Traveling outside of the US for the first time was thrilling, preparing for the trip to Russia meant getting my first passport. My life of adventure was racing full speed ahead. As we traveled throughout Russia I experienced the beauty of the country and the curiosity of the people. One older woman at a hotel we checked into, grasped my hand and rubbed my skin and said "Nice, Nice." I am not sure if she meant my skin color or my ethnicity, but she was friendly. Others stared or peeked out from behind newspapers. Children pointed. One incident was a little scary. A man walked around me a little too close for comfort. All in all the experience allowed me to appreciate another culture and be even more grateful for the diversity of culture in America and the freedom we live under. Later I would come to understand Philippians 3:20 at a deeper level; But our citizenship is in heaven. And we eagerly await a savior from there, the Lord Jesus Christ. Being a citizen of America is great but being a citizen of heaven is priceless. Where does your citizenship exist?

I learned a lot about music and vocal performance at UM, and enjoyed some social life as well. It was here that I pledged with Zeta Phi Beta Sorority. My mom and Aunt Ruth are/were also Zetas. (Ruth passed away on Dec. 31, 1999.) I was surrounded by wonderful women who were Zetas as well throughout my early years. Their example of service and support for each other and for the community provided positive role models for me, and I was thrilled to become a part of the sisterhood. The sorority would later assist me in traveling and studying abroad. I have many fond memories of pledging and of serving the community during my undergraduate years.

My first serious relationship with a boy developed during this time as well. He was a singer as well, with a beautiful baritone voice. He came from Washington, DC and I got a chance to visit his family there during that time. We both moved on to grad school and lost contact. He was a great guy who respected me and my desire to focus on my singing career and maintain a pure relationship. Oh, that I would have maintained those convictions! More about that later...

My first paying job as a singer began during this time. I was hired as an artist-in-residence at Kendall United Methodist Church in Kendall, Florida. It was the first of many jobs singing for different congregations, Christian and Jewish.

I was able to perform with the Miami Opera Guild chorus during this time, working with many great singers. I remember the performance of Samson and Delilah with heldentenor Jon Vickers, but it is not a pleasant memory. At the last rehearsal before the opening, he got very angry about one of the dancers moving during the banquet (orgy) scene. He threatened to kick the dancer if he moved again during his aria. I learned then the negative side of being an opera diva/divo. He went overboard, and it was ugly. My memories of the other performances are positive and I learned a lot about stage performance from being involved with a professional opera company.

I was also privileged to attend the Interlochen Music Camp one summer during my time at UM That was a wonderful experience which allowed me to work with Robert Shaw, one of the top choral conductors of that time.

I was also able to work with Willis Patterson, a well-known African-American voice teacher from the University of Michigan. My life opened up in ways I could never have imagined.

For my senior year, I took over 20 credits one semester, and prepared for my senior recital. My recital went very well and I made the President's Honor Roll (straight A's) during my last semester. I had always made the Dean's List, but this was amazing. I graduated magna cum laude from UM and went on to a full scholarship at Cincinnati Conservatory of Music. I had begun to travel outside of the box and loved it! Life was about to get more interesting–as well as dangerous.

Lessons Learned
Great vocal technique and performing skills
Professional stage skills
How to work hard and delay gratification
How to play and live a balanced life

Traveling opens and expands our minds and hearts
Music is truly the universal language
God always has a plan

To Do

Journal about experiences that took you outside of your box (your community, culture, etc.).

Chapter 3 – CCM/Europe

The proverbs of Solomon... for gaining wisdom and instruction; for understanding words of insight;... **Proverbs 1:1-10**
For I know the plans I have for you,... plans to prosper you and not to harm you, plans to give you hope and a future.
Jeremiah 29:11

Ending up in Cincinnati at the Conservatory of Music instead of New York at Manhattan School of Music, was one of many changes in my plans that would happen throughout my life. God always directs our path, even when we think we are running the show. The opportunity to acquire my masters degree on a full scholarship was a blessing and the selection of the director of the Kenner Program, Mrs. Lois Gordon. She chose me to be her graduate assistant and allowed me to continue my journey out of the box.

My first year at CCM was amazing. I auditioned for the main stage production of Benjamin Britten's *Albert Herring* and was selected for the role of Mrs. Wordsworth. I had just performed the same role my senior year at the University of Miami. Coincidence? I think not. The opera program gave me the opportunity to learn roles from *The Secret Marriage*, *Don Giovanni* and *Gianni Schicci*. I developed in so many ways as an artist, and I learned a hard lesson about breaking barriers and being a catalyst to help others to step out of the box.

After I completed my Master of Music degree with cum laude honors I took a year off and continued to work on my vocal skills and to teach music. I was able to continue to be an artist-in-residence at Calvary Episcopal Church. I used this time to prepare to audition for the Artist Diploma in Opera program. I felt sure that I would gain entry, since my excellent work as a singer and student was known to the faculty and my work ethic was well known also. After my audition I waited for the lists to go up announcing those accepted into the program. The day came and I was devastated to learn that I had not been accepted. I returned home and cried out to God on my knees, wondering why I was rejected.

Mrs. Gordon, who was my supervisor when I was a graduate student, called me over to her home and gave me a history lesson on CCM. Although the world-famous opera singer Kathleen Battle had attended the school, she was not a part of the Artist Diploma program. I was surprised to learn that there had never been an African-American in the program. I had no idea that I was trying to make history.

Well, needless to say, the next few days would be an education I would never forget. I got a message from my vocal teacher asking me to audition again and to prepare something lyrical. I did as I was asked, and went to the second audition prepared to sing an aria from Fidelio. Mr. Tajo, the head of the

Opera Department, was there; he had been absent during my first audition. I found out later that he was the one who had come to my rescue. He asked why I was not on the list of those accepted into the Diploma program, and was told that those in attendance heard something in my audition that they felt disqualified me. He wanted to hear for himself. I informed them of my selection; then they asked if I could sing an aria that I knew but had not prepared for the audition. I was allowed to stand behind the accompanist to glance at the score for the words. After I finished, the person playing for me said to me, "Dian, I don't know what they are listening for, but that was beautiful."

After that second audition I was accepted into the Diploma program, the first African-American singer accorded that honor. I had broken down the barrier. Others followed, and I am grateful for the lessons I learned as I stepped out of the box at CCM. I cannot say for sure why I was rejected the first time but accepted after the second audition. After learning the history I was able to relate to the saying in the African-American community that we have to work twice as hard and be twice as good in order to be accepted.

I decided that I was going to do whatever it took to prove my worthiness. It was good to know that there are many who couldn't care less what color of skin a singer has. A beautiful voice has no color, music is universal, and creating beautiful music is a gift given to all cultures and ethnicities. I am grateful that I was able to continue my education and perfect my craft as an opera singer.

After I finished the Artist Diploma, I traveled to Europe for more training at the AIMS institute in Graz, Austria. This was a time of great travel experiences, amazing vocal and language instruction--as well as a rude awakening about the classical music world.

I had the opportunity to work with a vocal coach from the Munich Opera. She asked me to turn off my tape recorder after I sang, "Ach, Ich Fuls" from The Magic Flute by Mozart. She then informed me that even though I sang it beautifully I should not audition with that aria while in Germany because it was a "German role." Blond hair and blue eyes I did not have. Once again the color of my skin was determining how I would or would not be accepted performing certain operatic roles. It was a hard lesson, but I kept working and was determined not to let anything deter me from my goal of becoming a professional singer.

As I think back on this time in my life I remember the hurt and puzzlement I felt as I maneuvered thru the minefield of what seemed like discrimination. I had to decide how to handle the injustice. It may have been my first experience but it would not be my last. Hebrews 12:15 is the verse that speaks to how to deal with any hurt or wound. "See to it that no one falls short of the grace of God and that no bitter root grows up to cause trouble and defile many." Bitterness destroys from the inside out. It does not allow you to move forward. It enslaves your mind, heart and spirit and poisons all around you. Anger is one of the byproducts and so is a lack of trust of people. When I think about the injustice Jesus dealt with and how he handled it. I understand that forgiveness is the only cure. Is there an injustice you need to deal with? Use Jesus as your example and go for the cure.

I learned many lessons during this time in my life. I made decisions that went contrary to my expressed value system of being a Christian. The choices I made in different situations could have led to tragedy. Looking back I wonder, "How could I have been so stupid?" The saying goes, "God protects babies and fools." Needless to say, I was no baby!

I met my first husband during this time and for a while all seemed to be going well. An opera singer and a jazz musician, a musical match made in heaven.... More on that later....

Lessons Learned:

The sky is the limit, regardless of the prejudices of others, as long as you are willing to work hard and persevere
Choices have consequences and rewards
There are many who see talent, skill and intelligence over skin color
When God opens a door no man can close it

To Do:
Journal about some your choices and the choices of others, and how they have affected you.

Chapter 4 – New York

.... "The God who made the world and everything in it is the Lord of heaven and earth and does not live in temples built by hands... God did this so that men would seek him and perhaps reach out for him and find him, though he is not far from each one of us. **Acts 17:22-31**

This scripture in Acts makes it so clear that God determines the exact times and places in our lives to allow us the opportunity to find him. After returning from Europe I lived in Miami for a while in preparation for my marriage to my first husband. He was (and still is) a very talented jazz saxophonist. We met while he was an undergraduate at the University of Miami's School of Music (my alma mater) and I was in his hometown working on my master's degree in music at CCM. We were introduced by a mutual friend, and the rest is history. We shared a passion for music and were both very talented in our areas of musical gifts.

We were engaged for five years before we decided to get married after we finished our degrees. He received his Bachelors of Music, and I completed my Masters in Music and the Artist Diploma in opera. We set the date for May 1986. I worked as a substitute teacher for Miami-Dade County Schools and continued to sing recitals and concerts as we prepared to move to New York.

The wedding went off without a hitch. We were newlyweds pursuing our dreams of becoming professional musicians. We arrived in Brooklyn after our wedding, moving into the Clinton Hill neighborhood. Our first year was spent working as substitute teachers, taking lessons and coaching sessions as we auditioned for various gigs. My husband (whom I will call JM for Jazz Man to respect his privacy) was playing on the weekends in the parks and subways of Manhattan.

It was a time of adventure and hard work. We were laying the foundation for our careers and enjoying life in the city as newlyweds. We were excited about seeing our dreams come true. JM landed his first gig with a big band and then later began touring with the Ray Charles Orchestra. I was beginning to work with different vocal music companies and began doing recitals in New York, New Jersey, St. Louis, Washington, DC, Cincinnati and Miami.

For the first three years, our marriage seemed to be going well. We were not interested in having kids at the time; all of our focus was on our music careers. We bought a condo and continued to pursue our careers. During this time I joined a local church congregation and continued to follow my family tradition of church on Sunday and weekly involvement with the youth and music ministries.

I began to desire more spiritual growth and prayed specifically to find a group of people who were just living out the scriptures. I had become disappointed with the lack of honesty and authenticity of my local ministry; I wanted to be challenged to grow spiritually and wanted to see the scriptures come alive in my life and the lives of others.

Up to this point I considered myself to be a Christian and was very committed to the ministry of Jesus. However, from the time I left my parents' home to go to college my way of life had gradually gone against the standard that all those who follow Christ should live by, laid out in the Bible. The wheels had come off during my graduate school years--the compromising, the sexual immorality, the deceit, the selfishness, the pride, the conflict-avoiding--and the list goes on. I was set on a collision course for disaster.

I had grown up singing in many different denominational churches. I had become weary with all that I had seen and experienced. I was beginning to believe that maybe it was not possible to live out the scriptures; maybe it was just an ideal that could not be a reality.

In March 1989, I decided to visit the midweek daytime ministry of the New York City church of Christ. I had been invited before, but this time the invite came from a young aspiring opera singer like me. We were both attending a master class at the 92nd Street Y. She invited me out to a Bible talk at Julliard, but my schedule would not allow me to come. I finally made it to the midweek service after she called several more times. I was blown away by what I experienced, and decided to attend the house church that Sunday. I liked what I heard and began studying the Bible with someone from the church later that week.

Over the next month God revealed himself to me like never before. I saw things in the scriptures I had never seen, and saw myself as I had never seen myself before. Many questions I had were answered and I was being challenged to change and grow, as I had prayed. It was not an easy process--I fought seeing the truth about myself, but ultimately the scriptures were clear. The Bible that I knew was true and reasonable had now transformed my life. God had determined the exact time and place for me to step out of my religious-tradition box and make Jesus Lord of my life. My life was turned upside down and would never be the same!

As you might expect, my marriage during this time was showing signs of stress. My husband was often out on the road, and when he would return he was distant and distracted. As I began to make Jesus Lord, and not music, he was not happy. He was still pursuing his career, and so was I, but my value system had changed, which created tension and arguments.

About a year and a half after I was baptized into Christ, I was in a terrible car accident. The car was totaled, and I was left to recover from a broken rib and a bruised body. JM was touring with Ray Charles in Europe. He stayed home for a week to make sure I was okay and settled with help from my sisters in Christ, and then returned to the tour.

A month or so later I received the phone call that would forever alter my life and marriage. My husband informed me over the phone that he had had an affair while on tour. I was already in physical pain, and now I was in the worst emotional pain of my life. I thought that my marriage would get better after I became a disciple of Christ, not worse. God was about to teach me some lessons about betrayal, trust and forgiveness.

Finding out about the infidelity of my husband was my first big emotional trauma. I had experienced the deaths of my grandparents and young cousins, but this was a different pain. I remember asking my mom one day about expectations of fidelity in marriage, and her answer to me was, "Only God deserves all of our hearts because only He is always faithful."

The combination of physical pain from the car accident and emotional pain from his infidelity brought me to a very low point emotionally. I remember thinking one day as I was soaking in my tub to ease the pain in my body that I could just slip under the water and be pain-free. Although it was a fleeting thought, it allowed me to better understand those who suffer from depression and suicidal thoughts. The directive from the scriptures to take every thought captive and make it obedient to Christ (2 Corinthians 10:5) became real.

Once JM returned from touring, we sought counseling and began trying to rebuild the relationship. He started studying the Bible, and I thought we were finally going to be able to be united in Christ. It was not to be; more infidelity followed, more lies were uncovered and the marriage ended. I was devastated and felt like a failure. I also wrestled with God as I worked through forgiving JM from my heart. Once I saw my own sin and shortcomings in the marriage, and the lies, deceit and sexual immorality that led up to the marriage, it was clear to me that a relationship not built God's way and nurtured God's way is doomed to fail.

I had to take responsibility for my choices and remember also that the ground is level at the foot of the cross. Jesus died for the forgiveness of all my sins how could I do any less for JM? First I made the decision to forgive, and then the Holy Spirit worked within me to enable me to forgive JM from the heart.

Forgiveness is something we all need on a daily basis. However when traumatic pain is involved there has to be a willingness to dig deep and discover what lies at the heart of the wound. For me, I had to revisit how my marriage to JM developed. Our "courtship" was worldly and immoral. There was deceit on both our parts. I was claiming to be a Christian but was not living by the standard of God's word. I had compromised so much leading up to this time and continued to do so. The foundation of our relationship was not built on truth; so once I was able to acknowledge this it was clear why it fell apart because of lies and betrayal. I had made a decision to build on a lie and was dealing with the consequence of that decision. Once I saw this I was able to see me and JM at the foot of the cross both in need of God's forgiveness. Matthew 6:15 makes it clear, if I couldn't forgive JM for sinning against me I would not be forgiven for sinning against God. In comparison my sins were far greater against God. This truth allowed my heart to open and humble out and ultimately forgive JM from the heart. The power of the Holy Spirit triumphed! Are there any areas of your heart that need some work when it comes to forgiveness? If so go for it, it will be well worth it. Thank God for the freedom that comes from a heart free of bitterness.

Lessons Learned:
Accomplishing your dreams takes hard work and perseverance
The Bible is right--the house built on sand will be destroyed when the storms come. (Matthew 7:24-27)
Forgiving from the heart is not easy, but it is essential if we are to remain whole from the inside out, as well as forgiven by God our Father and Jesus our Redeemer.

To Do: Journal about an experience that has called or is calling you to forgive from the heart.

_____
_____
_____
_____
_____
_____
_____
_____
_____
_____
_____
_____
_____
_____
_____

Chapter 5– New York - New Beginning

Trust in the Lord with all your heart and lean not on your own understanding; in all your ways submit to him and he will make your paths straight. **Proverbs 3:5-6**

God proved Himself to be real and trustworthy to me as I made the decision to trust Him with my life, beginning a new direction as a single woman again. By the time my divorce was final I was working full-time in the ministry for the New York City church of Christ. My life was full of teaching, discipling and studying the Bible with women from diverse backgrounds and cultures. I saw once again that there is only one race, the human race. All human beings have the same need for redemption and love. I enjoyed sharing my life lessons and learning from the lives of the women I was serving as we lived out being partners in the gospel.

Several months later, I began leading a portion of the Brooklyn ministry of the church with a young disciple from the Queens ministry of the NYC church. His name was Kendall Knight, Jr. He was seven years my junior in physical age and five years my junior as a disciple. At the time we began leading together, we had gone on two dates--and we were about to begin an adventure.

Kendall and I began leading an Arts ministry for the Brooklyn Region of the church during the fall of 1994. We worked well together and began building a great friendship. We both continued to date other disciples, but by spring of the following year we were dating steadily.

Kendall showed himself to be an amazingly perceptive man. He was upfront and direct. What you saw is what you got and that was refreshing for me. I was wounded by the deceit in my previous marriage and I needed someone who could be trusted. Kendall was that man. He would show me that over and over again during our marriage and I was feeling very blessed by God choosing him for me.

By the end of the summer we were engaged and headed off to South Africa for a ministry leaders' conference. This was the trip of a lifetime for both of us. Visiting the continent of Africa for the first time was an emotional one for both of us and for several other African-Americans who were part of our leadership staff. Our ancestors were from this continent and had been taken by force to America and the West Indies. Now we were returning as free men and women socially and, more importantly, spiritually. It was an amazing trip. We learned a lot from the seminar and experienced a safari for the first time. Our lives were full of adventure and learning. We were excited about building our lives and our ministry together.

Once we returned we set a December date for our wedding, and continued to work together building the ministry in Brooklyn. We were married on December 16, 1995. We honeymooned on a cruise to Key West and Mexico. This was my first honeymoon even though it was my second marriage. My relationship with Kendall was a pure one. Our first night of physical intimacy was on the wedding night! God's way is really the best way. I know now from experience that the self-control and self-denial you establish during the dating process prepares you for living out these essential disciplines in your marriage. Married life calls for a deeper level of self-control and self-denial, since you are bringing together two lives complete with baggage--good, bad and ugly. Even though we were both disciples who had made the commitment to make Jesus Lord of our lives, we still had to grow in learning how to live that out in a marriage. We are still doing that today. Becoming a disciple of Christ is a journey, not a destination.

Our first year of marriage was wonderful and exciting! We continued to serve the ministry in Brooklyn and travel the world for leadership seminars. We visited Los Angeles and the Dominican Republic. We dealt with some deaths in Kendall's family (uncles on his father's side) but nothing would prepare us for the roller coaster to follow.

Because I was 37 by the time we married, we waited only a year before trying to get pregnant. We tried for about six months and then decided to go to a fertility specialist, since I was 38 by then. We were both tested to see if there was any physical reason why we were not able to conceive. There was none, so we tried several fertility treatments but nothing worked.

It was a very emotional time for me; I was having a hard time surrendering to God's plan. There was a reason He was saying "no" to us having a biological child. I would find out that reason later, but during that time I had to learn to trust God and follow His lead.

We had always wanted to have a child and adopt a child so we began the adoption process with an organization called HOPE for Children during the summer of 1998. We sent in our profiles with pictures of us and our interests, did our home studies and other paper work, and waited for the call. The first opportunity was a sibling group. They were 2 years and several months old. We decided to wait for just one infant. The next opportunity was an infant all right--two to be exact! They were twin boys, born October 12, who needed a home. We had applied to adopt one child, but God was making it clear it would be two. Kendall was fired up but I needed to pray. Zero to one overnight is one thing, but zero to two was going to be an adventure! Our marriage started as an adventure and our lives were continuing that trend.

We accepted the opportunity to adopt the twins and the adventure began. The agency was having a hard time finding the birth father to have him sign over his parental rights. We were advised not to go to Atlanta (the boys were born in Marietta, just outside of Atlanta) until that paperwork was completed. In addition to this we found out that the mother was in the first stage of syphilis. This meant that the boys could have been infected and could develop blindness as result of passing through the birth canal. If the doctors had known ahead of time they could have done a C-section. Tests were performed and the boys were given antibiotics for ten days in the hospital. Everything turned out fine and the boys were healthy. It was now November and the agency was still trying to contact the birth father. I remember asking God one Sunday that if these were the boys he wanted us to raise and nurture, to please allow the birth father to be found by Friday and for him to sign the papers. God answered that prayer with a resounding "yes." We got the call on Friday. They found the birth father and he signed the papers.

We were thrilled to travel to Atlanta on November 9th and meet our sons for the first time in the home of their foster parents. The foster parents gave us our instructions for the evening and threw us into the water. We were up twice that evening but did well that first night. It was an amazing time. We were new parents of twin boys, Joshua and Caleb and felt so blessed by God to have the joy of nurturing these boys into adulthood and beyond!

We returned from Atlanta and were met at the airport by friends and family. Our ministry had thrown us a baby shower before we left, so we had everything we needed and the nursery was ready. The couple who served as elders for our ministry in Brooklyn came home with us and watched the boys for the first night so that we could get a good night's sleep. They had raised three kids of their own and were also grandparents by then. We were very grateful for their help. The campus girls volunteered to help and many friends pitched in as well. We were off on a great adventure and life was exciting!

Our first year as a family was full of adventure. We were serving the Brooklyn ministry, leading the region which included three groups of about 200 adults and 75 to 80 children. We were busy but enjoying every moment. We were expecting to take the ministry into the year 2000. It was not to be. We had been told that adopting the twins could affect how we would continue to serve in the full-time ministry. The decision was made for us to come out of Brooklyn and go to Queens. It was an emotional time for us; we felt that the move was not going to be good for the Brooklyn ministry since so many young leaders had just been put in place. We shared our concerns with those who were making the decision, but the decision was made to move us to another ministry anyway. All of the issues we feared would develop came to pass. The faith of many disciples was hurt and damaged. We were eventually able to talk and reconcile our hurt with those who made the decision and learned that God is sovereign. Lessons were learned across our fellowship and we are all wiser because of it. God's timing is perfect and his plans can never be thwarted. We made the move to Queens and did our best to jump in and serve the ministry there. Kendall was returning to the ministry where he was converted and it was a time to reconnect with those earlier relationships.

Moving to Queens opened the next door of challenges that God was calling us to walk through. Soon after we moved into our home in Forest Hills, Queens I began to notice that my right hand was not steady. I was having involuntary tremors off and on. My vision was also blurring off and on. One of my closest friends suggested I see a neurologist. My grandfather was diagnosed with Parkinson's disease late in life so I thought maybe it could be the early stages of that illness. I went to the doctor and he sent me to have an MRI; when the results came back, he called me in to give me the diagnosis. He started off by saying, "I have good news and bad news." I replied, "Give me the good news first." He said, "The good news is you don't have Parkinson's, but the bad news is you may have multiple sclerosis." I was in shock. I never thought that this was a possibility. I remember walking down the street after that office visit and talking with God: "Well, Father, I guess these are the cards you are dealing for me." The next six months were a whirlwind of different doctors and many tests. I learned as much as I could about the disease and prepared to deal with my new reality. I found out during this time that if I had become pregnant it could have caused the disease to progress rapidly. God had protected me by preventing us from having a biological child. Needless to say, my trust and faith in God grew to a whole new level. I learned that when God says "no" or "wait," He is doing what is best for us no matter how we may feel about it. As the song says, "We'll understand it better by and by."

I began treatment for MS using a once a week injection and continued to try working full-time in the ministry. Kendall and I moved forward prayerfully, trying to decide if it was the best thing for me to continue working full-time. After much prayer and lots of advice, we decided to resign from full-time ministry. Kendall returned to the corporate world and I focused on learning to live with MS.

We looked for a home to purchase in Queens and Long Island and in the midst of that, the country went through the worst attack of my lifetime: 9/11! Two planes crashed into the World Trade Center towers, and one each into the Pentagon and a field in Pennsylvania. Later it would be reported, that plane was headed for the capital or the White House! Kendall was working a block and a half away from the World Trade Center and I was at home watching it all unfold on TV. I spoke with Kendall as the first tower was falling. He had to get off the phone and I did not hear from him for three hours. I was a mess and called a close friend to have her pray with me. One of my friends was over helping me with the boys. She was supposed to be at the restaurant at the top of one of the towers that day. The event was canceled and her life was spared. All those at the top of the towers perished that day.

When Kendall was finally able to call he was fine but had to walk from downtown Manhattan to the 59th Street Bridge and then walk across to get the subway home. He was tired and covered with dust from the debris of the fallen towers, but he was okay. So many people lost family members that day-- I was very grateful that God protected him.

Learning to trust is rooted in our experiences from infancy and childhood. My life as an infant and child was full of stability, nurturing and love. As a result I responded to life trusting people and circumstances until they gave me a reason not to do so. Putting Prov. 3:5-6 into practice was not easy as I dealt with all of the situations during this time of my life, but God had been preparing me for this flood of challenges from childhood. I have learned that my journey of faith has been under God's care from my mother's womb through childhood, adolescence, young adulthood and adulthood as a single woman, a married woman and now a mother of twin boys. As I trusted God through every challenge, disappointment, injustice, hurt and victory I have developed a faith that is rooted deep in the sovereignty and love of my heavenly Father. The peace that I live in now comes from putting into practice Philippians 4:4-7 "Rejoice in the Lord always, I will say it again; Rejoice! Let your gentleness be evident to all. The Lord is near. Do not be anxious about anything, but in every situation, by prayer and petition, with Thanksgiving, present your requests to God. And the peace of God, which transcends all understanding, will guard your hearts and your minds in Christ Jesus."

By December of 2001 we had decided to move to Atlanta and found a great home there for our family. We knew many families who had moved to Atlanta from our ministry in New York so it was a good choice for us. We were working through some disappointments about how our exit from the ministry was handled, and it was encouraging to be among families we knew well. We settled into our new home and ministry and continued to work through all the challenges our new lives. God is faithful; He helped us to heal and forgive and grow in grace. We are all still being transformed into the likeness of Christ as disciples of Jesus. God is always calling us out of our comfort zones and asking us to step out of our familiar boxes. It is never pleasant at the time but it is always worth the growth that comes as a result.

Lessons Learned:
Life is full of adventure--the good, the bad and the tragic
God comforts us through all of our hurts, disappointments and losses
Specific and surrendered prayers are an opportunity to see God more clearly
God is faithful and worthy of all of our trust; He will never forsake us or forget us.

To Do:
Journal about some of the challenges, losses or hurts God has comforted you through.

Chapter 6 –Atlanta

Therefore we do not lose heart. Though outwardly we are wasting away, yet inwardly we are being renewed day by day... **2 Corinthians 4:16-18**

I love this scripture in 2 Corinthians 4. It has helped me to put my illness in the right perspective. Our move to Atlanta was prompted by the benefits of the climate and the relationships that would be our support as we dealt with our new challenges. I was able to go to the Shepherd Center in downtown Atlanta; they have an MS center which is one of the best in the country. Working with the staff there I was able to learn to deal with my loss as a result of the MS. My medication was changed, and subsequent MRIs showed no progression of the disease.

I began to teach private voice lessons and eventually returned to teaching part-time at a Gwinnett County Charter School. It was now time for me to use all of the talent, training and performance experience from my music education to give back to the community and my ministry. Kendall and I were able to build the music ministry for one of the Atlanta area ministries, and then move on to work with the Arts and Entertainment Ministry in Atlanta through the Greater Atlanta church of Christ.

Our time in Atlanta has also brought new challenges, tragedies and victories. One of the first was the suicide of Kendall's brother, a New York City police officer. His life had spiraled out of control and he decided to end his life rather than surrender to God. It was a very painful time for our family, and Kendall was filled with sadness because his brother refused the spiritual help that he offered many times. We learned during this time that we can love and offer life through Christ to family and friends but it is up to them to choose life! Thankfully we have seen my youngest sister and Kendall's mom respond to the gospel by repenting and being baptized for the forgiveness of their sins. They chose life and are now helping others to do the same.

God is still revealing his plans for our lives. I have joined the 50's club and life is good! We are grateful that He has allowed Kendall and me to earn enough to send Joshua and Caleb to one of the top private Christian schools in the Southeast and enable others to do so as well. I am also able to teach at their school in the School of Music after-school program. My health has stabilized and I am eating in a healthy manner and working out consistently to maintain the state of remission of my MS.

My journey of faith has been full of valleys, hills and mountaintop experiences. As I surrendered to God's direction along the way he has guided me to the path he desires for me. As I trusted Him he has given me the desires of my heart. Psalm 16:6 says it best; "The boundary lines have fallen for me in pleasant places; surely I have a delightful inheritance." Are you surrendering to God's guidance? He is ready and waiting to give you the desires of your heart.

God is truly faithful in all He does in our lives. I have come a long way from Liberty City, Miami. God has called me over and over again to step out of the box in every area of my life. I pray to continue to be obedient to His calls and to spend the rest of my life helping others to do that as well. To God be all the glory for the things He has done and will do in my life to come!

Lessons learned so far:
All of life's challenges are to refine us into the likeness of Christ
God will always comfort us through life's pains
Surrendering to God is always worth it, no matter how painful it may be at the time

To Do:
Journal about the boxes God has called or is calling you out of.

_____
_____
_____
_____
_____
_____
_____

New York

University of Miami

Early Years

Atlanta

CCM/EUROPE

New York: New Beginnings